10599136

Listen to the Quiet

The Gentle Art of Nourishing Your Soul

Alda Ellis

Harvest House Publishers
Eugene, Oregon

*Dedicated to my loving husband, who
has supported me through the stresses
of life and encouraged moments
of listening to the quiet.*

Listen to the Quiet
Copyright © 2000 by Alda Ellis
Published by Harvest House Publishers
Eugene, OR 97402

Library of Congress Cataloging-in-Publication Data
Ellis, Alda, 1952-
    Listen to the quiet / Ellis.
        p. cm.
        ISBN 0-7369-0217-1
          1. Women—Conduct of life. I. Title.
    BJ1610 .E56 1999
    248.8'43—dc21
                     99-043334

Artwork which appears in this book is from
the personal collection of Alda Ellis.

Design and production by Left Coast Design, Portland, Oregon.

All rights reserved. No portion of this book may be reproduced
in any form without the written permission of the Publisher.

Printed in China.

00 01 02 03 04 05 06 07 08 09 / PP / 10 9 8 7 6 5 4 3 2 1

Contents

Listen to the Quiet

In the midst of our busy day-to-day schedules, it is so easy to get caught up in the world's hectic pace. We're told that our lives today are much better because of the high-speed, high-tech convenience of modern inventions—cell phones, commuter travel, fax machines, e-mail, and the like. Yet with life moving at such a rapid pace, is it any wonder we feel scattered and stressed?

In a world where being called an overachiever or a perfectionist is considered a compliment, we sometimes feel guilty if we take a moment for ourselves. But should we feel this way? It is with great comfort that I turn to the pages of the Bible for an answer. There I am given an example of what to do when I find myself overwhelmed by life. I read about Jesus going up to the mountain to pray all by Himself. He knew that He needed to fill up His well before His spring could flow out and pour blessings onto those around Him. Likewise, when we are healthy and happy on the inside, it radiates outward to our families, to our friends, and to the world around us.

This book is a gentle celebration of the art of renewing our souls as we learn to unwind and find peace and comfort—all without a note of guilt. I hope you'll be inspired to find your own favorite ways to take time for yourself and savor the rewards of the quiet.

An eighth-century philosopher once said, "Look in the perfumes of flowers and of nature for peace of mind and joy of life." In today's terms, that simply means we must take time to smell the roses. I smile and imagine that this philosopher was not juggling motherhood, a business, and a household as we do. In this dawning of a new century, such is the fast-paced life of ours. As a result, we need more than ever for our cups to be filled with renewed energy and passion.

It is very difficult for some of us to take time for ourselves. I confess that I have the "keep everybody happy" personality. It is hard for me to stop and take time for myself. However, I do think that I have gathered a few secrets along the way. Here I share with you my own ideas and inspirations for finding, listening to, and nurturing the quiet within your soul.

The nurturing of the soul can mean different things to different people. It can mean sneaking in a cozy Sunday afternoon nap, throwing clay on a potter's wheel, sipping hot chocolate while reading by the fireside, lingering over a late evening meal, or planting a row of cheerful pansies along the walk. The activity might sound merely ordinary, but the results of engaging in the activity are extraordinary.

When I have been traveling for days at a time—shuffling meetings, schedules, and layovers, hailing taxis, and waiting in long lines at restaurants—it is so comforting to come home. I leave my bags on the doorstep and take a quiet walk around our lake, where I revel in the colors, sounds, and scents of the outdoors. If I am lucky, I have the company of a little boy, my loving husband, or a welcoming Labrador retriever as I walk. Hearing the crunch of leaves under my feet before I even unzip my suitcase brings me back to where I am the happiest and most content.

There is a need in all of us to replenish and restore what we have given to those around us. We need to be reassured that it is just fine to spend moments alone reflecting upon our own dreams and goals, especially when it is our nature to keep everyone else content and think of ourselves last. At

Give me my scallop-shell of quiet,
My staff of faith to walk upon,
My scrip of joy, immortal diet,
My bottle of salvation,
My gown of glory, hope's true gage,
And thus I'll take my pilgrimage.

SIR WALTER RALEIGH

these times we must step back and realize how important it is to keep our wells filled with renewing water. This water spills out through our daily actions to nourish others.

I truly believe that the Creator has planted seeds of greatness in all of us. We must nurture these seeds. It is with this in mind that I share with you gentle ways to nurture the wellsprings of your soul. You will become happy, content, and more productive, which will bring joy to those you love and enrich the lives of those who surround you.

Listen to the Solitude

*In solitude we give passionate attention
to our lives, to our memories,
to the details around us...*

VIRGINIA WOOLF
A ROOM OF ONE'S OWN

I love to observe my son's fifth-grade teacher standing in front of twenty-six noisy, chattering students as she captures their attention at the beginning of the school day. Amid the morning excitement, Mrs. Lieb walks to the front of the classroom and starts to speak in a loving, quiet voice. The children in the front row desks politely shush the others so all can hear what their teacher is saying. Ears perk up to listen as she orderly begins a new day of enriching children's lives. The fifth-graders need to be quiet and listen before they can learn. So, too, must we.

...attain the grace of silence.

HARRIET
BEECHER
STOWE

My favorite way to start a new day is with a morning walk. The beginning of my walk reminds me of a painter's empty canvas. With each step I

A Daily Dose of Solitude

Like getting plenty of water and exercise, building solitude into your day is good for you. What activities have a relaxing and calming effect on you? Choose one to engage in each day and make a daily appointment with yourself to listen to solitude. Here are some favorite ways to reward yourself with a daily dose of solitude—

- *Reading a daily devotional*
- *Writing in a journal*
- *Playing or listening to music*
- *Reading a classic book*
- *Spending time in prayer*
- *Taking a morning or evening walk*
- *Writing a letter to a friend*
- *Listening to the sound of the outdoors*
- *Sketching or painting*
- *Enjoying a cup of tea*

imagine how I wish to paint my day. It always must include the background of necessary appointments and responsibilities, but to that I add the decorative flourishes of the dreams and wishes of my heart. A morning jaunt is my time to reflect, appreciate my life, and count my blessings. It is a time for me to be motivated, inspired, and encouraged.

Reading a morning devotion always rewards me, both spiritually and physically. Good management of your day always begins with a good planning session, and who better to help you plan than God? After spending time communing with Him, I feel refreshed and energized, anticipating whatever is to come.

When the three-thirty school bell rings, most of the time my schedule allows me to be in the car waiting for my youngest son, Samuel, to come bursting out of his classroom. I try to arrive at the school ten or so minutes early in order to spend a bit of time in solitude, eyes closed. Taking just a few minutes

The morning, which is the most memorable season of the day. . . Morning is when I am awake and there is a dawn in me. . .

HENRY DAVID THOREAU

to calm my mind readies my spirit to receive my family back home at the end of the day. If I can have just a moment to myself, I am much more patient and attentive when listening to others. We all need to establish our own rituals that help us to unwind and relax at the end of a busy day.

I love to share my

own hopes, dreams, and aspirations within the pages of a journal. A moment journaling alone is one of my favorite opportunities for quiet and reflection—no matter when it is worked into my day.

With pen in hand and pages spread open, I enjoy expressing ideas and thoughts that help to relieve my daily worries and concerns. In the corner of my bedroom sits a small writing table and chair. I have dedicated that space to the pursuit of writing. The cubbyholes on the desk are filled with pretty papers, note cards, floral stickers, and my journal. A cut-crystal water glass holds freshly sharpened pencils and smooth-writing pens. I also love to display blooming flowers on my little desk. From an African violet planted in a teacup to a fistful of wildflowers my son has picked, flowers make any space seem so much more charming. In my own little creative space, I can sit down and look forward to the joy of writing.

I believe that people who lived in eras past had more quiet time to themselves than we have now. They lived before the distractions of television, computers, and videos. Slipping outside to relax on the porch or lounge under a shade tree was the norm. After the dinner dishes were hand-washed and dried, there was a natural quieting down of the evening. I try to achieve that, but I still consider it a little luxury when I *can* afford an after-dinner quiet time.

On occasion after

Tubside Pampering

Turn your bathtub into your own personal retreat to solitude.

- ✿ Artfully arrange large strawberries, melon balls, and purple grapes on a decorative platter. Add a piece or two of your favorite chocolate, then set the platter on the side of the tub and enjoy nibbling during your hot, soothing soak. Have a glass of ice water nearby garnished with lemon and mint.
- ✿ Play soothing music, preferably instrumental music, to keep your mind clear.
- ✿ Place a small vase of fresh flowers on the side of the tub so you can take in their beauty.
- ✿ Set the room aglow with candlelight.
- ✿ Prepare bath water with bath salts or foaming bath gel.
- ✿ Have a ready assortment of sponges, soaps, and oils on hand.
- ✿ Drape a big, fluffy bath towel nearby.

everyone is asleep, I sit on my front porch and enjoy the midnight breeze. Just listening to the sounds of the evening is a wonderful way to close my day. The crickets chirp, my old wooden porch swing creaks, sheer draperies whisper in the wind, and at times a spring thunder rolls. I also love to sit and listen to a summertime rainfall. The quenching pitter-patter of raindrops dancing on our green shingle roof is so soothing and comforting. I find it an ideal setting for listening to the quiet.

For some, playing a musical instrument is a quieting activity that brings peace and solitude. When I was a child, my mother wanted me to learn to play the piano. I, however, did not wish to learn. I dreaded the lessons. I imagine my teacher dreaded them, too. It was so hard to make myself practice during the week, and I kept a close watch on the thirty-minute timer atop the piano when I did sit down to play. But now I realize it *was* an important time to myself. I

A Box Full of Luxury

Even if you don't have room to set up a desk just for the luxury of journaling or letter writing, you can fill a gingham-covered shoebox with delightful papers, note cards, your journal, and writing instruments. Tie up the box with a pretty grosgrain ribbon so it will feel like you are indulging in a little luxury whenever you bring it out.

cherish those piano memories.

Now grown with children of my own, I longed to give my boys the gift of music but I didn't want it to be a chore. When each of my sons was just three years old, I enrolled them in Suzuki violin classes. Their teacher, Mr. McSpadden, lived a professional life of music, as he had studied the violin in Germany and now spent his summers traveling the world over, perform-ing and conducting

*Make it your ambition
to lead a quiet life.*

1 THESSALONIANS 4:11

seminars. He was a world-renowned musician and an incredible instructor.

The Art of the Nap

Take a few minutes out of your day especially for a refreshing nap. The following hints will help make your nap a renewing experience.

- Decide just how long you would like to nap. I suggest at least ten minutes, but perhaps no more than twenty. Too long a nap will simply make you feel groggy. It's best to trust yourself to wake up on time, but if you have an appointment set an alarm clock so you can drift into sleep without worrying you'll miss something important.

- Adjust the light in the room. If it is too bright, draw the curtains or pull the shades. If it is too dark, let a soft, restful light bathe the room.

- Get comfortable. Slip off your shoes and loosen your belt. Put your feet up.

- Lie down with a comfy quilt, afghan, or comforter, but do not crawl between the sheets. Save getting under the covers only for retiring at night or recovering from illness.

- Clear your mind, take a deep breath, and close your eyes.

- Upon awakening, open your eyes and collect your thoughts. Take a deep breath and appreciate how much better you now feel. Slide your shoes back on and readjust the light in the room. Fold the quilt or covering so you leave the room tidy as you walk away, feeling renewed and refreshed.

Mr. McSpadden has since
passed away, but his
teachings remain with us
still. He taught us that we
must first *listen* to the
music before we could
play it. Listening was the
most important part of
becoming a musician.
Mr. McSpadden's most
important advice was
to the parents: "Never
ask your children to *practice*, but encourage them
to *play!*" This has had a lifelong impression on my
oldest son, Mason, for now when he is worried
about something, he will pick up his violin. I
can hear the concern voiced in his music
as he plays. Meditative, relaxing,
and therapeutic, music is
nourishing to his soul.
Find a way today to
work the comfort of soli-
tude into your own life.
Take a moment to journal. Sit
on the porch at midnight.
Lose yourself in the playing
of music. Let the nurturing
quiet of solitude fill your heart.

Listen to Creativity

*Every artist dips his brush into his own soul,
and paints his own nature into his pictures.*

HENRY WARD BEECHER

A framed needlepoint tapestry of roses and birds is displayed in my hall as my reminder to listen to creativity. This needlepoint is a treasured heirloom to me because I worked on it lovingly, stitch by stitch, at my grandmother's bedside as she lay in a hospital bed some twenty years ago. Words between us were rarely spoken as she drifted in and out of consciousness, but one thing remained constant—she knew I was there by her side and that she was not alone. There were many things I could have been doing during that time, but somehow sitting quietly by her side satisfied my soul. My grandmother was a link to my past and provided a glimpse of where my family was going. I treasure the needlepoint tapestry, for it kept my hands busy as my heart listened to the quiet and I honored our time together.

My friend Mary works in a home office facing a computer screen most of the day. Her personal retreat is just a step beyond the office door to her

Restoring Yesterday's Creativity

I listen to quiet creativity when I head out on antiquing jaunts in the countryside. Here I receive inspiration to put old treasures to new uses. An antique fruit print, a jar of unique buttons, an oval glass with a gilded frame, or an autograph book dated 1912 all set my creativity to flowing. Displaying and arranging the polka-dot glasses and Jadeite dinnerware I collect help me to keep the hunt alive for undiscovered finds. I like to spend time in the midst of these treasures, allowing my mind to focus on the thrill of discovery. Visit an estate sale, an antique show, or your grandmother's attic to search for glassware, quilts, heirloom photographs, and other discoveries that will add yesterday's beauty to your life.

craft room where she, a talented flower arranger, creates beautiful floral baskets. There she weaves wreaths of dried roses and wildflowers together to dress a mantel, a window, or a frame. This is Mary's form of imaginative expression as she spends time in this special room designed for creative pursuits. "A little kingdom I possess, where thoughts and feelings dwell," wrote Louisa May Alcott in *Little Women*. For Mary, her little kingdom is the room she calls her own, a room she fills with crafting supplies, baskets, and flowers. This cherished space nourishes her creative soul.

We are all blessed with some form of artistic talent. It just may surface in different ways at different times in our lives. Years ago, before I had children, I took up oil painting. As a dental hygienist, I worked in a small office all day long. Painting was such a release of creative pleasure after the tedious and serious nature of my daily routine. I could be so tired from my day in the dental office, yet I always left my evening painting class refreshed and renewed.

Let us have a quiet hour...

ALFRED, LORD
TENNYSON

Painting was very important to me at the time, for it was my invitation to

tranquility. I lovingly called it my therapy and looked forward to every class. As we sipped Red Zinger tea from porcelain rose teacups, we were taught by a delightful English lady who looked at the world in the variegated hues of an oil painter's palette. I left her class with an oil painting in my hand and a renewed imagination in my heart.

Many eyes go through the meadow, but few see the flowers.

RALPH WALDO EMERSON

Creativity enables us to see our world in a new light. A collection of sable brushes gathered in a keepsake coffee cup and my father's old green tackle box filled with wrinkled, half-squeezed tubes of paint enabled me to create a canvas of lush, dew-kissed cabbage roses amid a bowl of fruit. I knew my scattering of cherry-hued blossoms would never hang in a museum as a celebrated masterpiece, but as each rose petal began to take form, the brush strokes painted a peace within me.

Today I do not have the time to get out my paints. Perhaps someday I will, but for now I am content to arrange a cluster of roses in a pretty teapot. Roses, with their graceful petals and abundant fragrance, always transform my world into a place of serenity.

Creativity and serenity enter into our lives when we invest time in making our hearts happy. While waiting in line at the grocery store one day, I heard two silver-haired ladies conversing. They had recently taken a knitting class together and one lady asked the other if she ever wore the sweater she had knitted in class. Her reply made me smile. "Heaven sakes, no!" she laughed. "The only reason I kept going to that class was because I enjoyed the company." It was not the sweater that had kept this

Let Your Creativity Blossom

Perhaps you don't consider yourself a painter, a writer, or a musician. But chances are, you possess many creative talents that you simply need to discover! Many community colleges and private organizations offer a variety of classes in the imaginative pursuits. Or buy a book and some supplies and teach yourself how to do something new. Here are some ideas to get you started—

- *Painting, drawing, watercolor*
- *Pottery, ceramics, sculpture*
- *Jewelry making*
- *Knitting, needlepoint, quilting*
- *Gardening, flower arranging*
- *Photography, videography*
- *Poetry, fiction writing, journaling*
- *Dancing, singing, playing an instrument*
- *Cooking, baking*
- *Scrapbooking, paper making*

A Gardening Spirit

Make easy garden markers with flat, unusual rocks and flagstones. Use a wide, permanent marker to record on the stones the names of the herbs and flowers in your garden. Garden markers add a touch of charm by personalizing your garden and are especially nice to show what has been planted in a perennial garden.

lady warm. Rather, it was the comfort of being surrounded by friends amid the gentle pull on strands of yarn. The creative stitches wove a sweater, but beyond that they wove the golden thread of friendship. The knitted sweater was but a symbol of the time she spent, needles clicking, nurturing her soul in the company of friends.

Not long ago I lost a member of my family who I was dearly close to, my beloved mother. I used to talk to her on a daily basis, as she and my father lived close by. This loss hurt not only me, but also all whose lives she had touched. It was felt most deeply by my eighty-six-year-old father. As a part of the healing process, I took time off of work and devoted it to being with him. And something beautiful came out of sharing our deep hurt—a sparkling stained-glass window.

My father and

I spent our mornings together, hearts aching like no words can express. But we decided to keep our hands occupied, and so began our creation of a leaded stained-glass window. Dad had spent a lifetime diligently working on projects as a carpenter. In our red barn, with his hands laboring alongside mine, we traced and cut the patterns, filed the brightly-colored glass, and leaded the seams. The painful readjustment of our lives slowly developed into a pattern of healing as our window took form. The beautiful finished product hangs in my office today as a precious reminder of the time Dad and I

spent together, hands kept busy, few words spoken,
hearts searching for hope. As light now shines
through the window we created out of our loss, I
realize that its true beauty lies in the memory of
time spent alone with my father as we listened to
the quiet.

I nurture quiet and creativity beside the small,
moss-lined stream that runs through my flower garden. I love the saying "One is nearer to God's heart in
the garden than anywhere else on earth." Listening
to the trickle of water falling on the rocks, pinching
spent flowerheads to encourage a profusion of
blooms, and caring for my beds of hostas and impa-
tiens is so soothing to me. The quiet artistry that the
garden lends with its colorful beauty and dash of
irresistible fragrance is nurturing to my soul.

The garden that you tend needn't be a tidy row

of seedlings or a fenced-in plot of grand propor-
tions. Even the simplest window boxes displayed
on a ledge in the city can greet passersby with
unmatchable fragrance and a sense of lushness.
Spring narcissus bulbs bursting forth in bloom,

cascading summer
petunias, and the rich
color of fall mums all
bring forth a season
of restoration. The
caretaking, feeding,
and watering of a
garden all your own
brings immense
pleasure to the senses
and is nourishing to the
soul. Take time to hear
the inspiring echoes of
creativity.

October is the month for painted
leaves. Their rich glow now flashes
round the world. These little leaves
are the stained glass windows in
the cathedral of my world.

HENRY DAVID THOREAU

Listen to Pampering

Nothing can cure the soul but the senses,
just as nothing can cure the
senses but the soul.

OSCAR WILDE

I love to introduce little luxuries into my daily life. When I indulge in these luxuries, I make a place in my life for the ritual of pampering. A restoring soak in a warm tub is a treat that I sometimes enjoy after everyone is asleep and all is quiet. When I spend time alone in the bath, I am able to do things I never have time for in the mornings—brushing my hair one hundred strokes, polishing my nails, applying a herbal facial mask, soaking my feet in a minty wash—while a fragranced candle flickers nearby. Here I take time to meditate, think, read, and perform little rituals of beauty that soothe my soul.

You really need just three things for a bath—water, soap, and a towel. But you can add so many niceties to soothe and pamper yourself. Candles, herbal teas, bath beads and bubbles, gels, and creams cleanse spirit as well as body. Delightfully fragrant, a handful of rose petals tossed into warm bath water along with a few drops of lavender

Scents that Make Sense

Essential oils come in a variety of scents and, beyond their luscious aroma, they have medicinal properties to help you feel your best. Some favorite essential oils and their refreshing effects are—

- **Chamomile**: mild and calming
- **Eucalyptus**: stimulating
- **Lavender**: calming for headaches and nervousness
- **Lemon**: antidepressant
- **Patchouli**: calming
- **Peppermint**: stimulating

essential oil create a lulling escape.

The bath is where all of the senses can be soothed as you feel the ripple of running water between your fingers and the warmth of miniature waves on your tired body. The fragrance of essential oils, the refreshing taste of a cup of tea, the playful sound of splashing water, and the soft light of

a scented candle can touch all of your senses and create a retreat for contemplating the day's events or letting your thoughts turn to daydreaming.

Fragrant oils and candles can naturally

Inside myself is a place where I live all alone and that's where you renew the springs that never dry up.

PEARL S. BUCK

soothe, uplift, and calm us. Thoughtfully placed about the room, candles create a mood of tranquility, just as the sound of running water helps to clear your thoughts. A comfortably warm bath moves you toward calmness and contentment, and you'll surely feel rested upon leaving the tub.

In the summer, a soothing soak is a welcome relief for tired and aching muscles. Here in the tub we can unwind from working in the garden, jogging or bicycling, or playing with lively children. Just watching and listening to the water and breathing in its freshness is the beginning to letting go of tension. And a summertime bath has its practical aspects, too. Add baking soda to cool water for relief from the itching of poison ivy, the sting of sunburn, or the discomfort of summer rashes.

*The day becomes
more solemn and serene
When noon is past—
there is a harmony
In autumn, and a
lustre in its sky...*

PERCY BYSSHE SHELLEY

Winter is an especially good time for a long, hot soak, for it is the season of colds and allergies. One or two drops of eucalyptus oil added to the water and a cup of honey-laced tea to sip

help to
ease
the
symp-
toms of
winter. The
steam from
fragrant
eucalyptus
water opens the
sinuses and the
honeyed tea
soothes a
scratchy throat.
    Besides
tasting delicious,
a cup of tea has
many health bene-
fits. For 4,000 years people
have been drinking tea
and singing its praises as it
helps prevent disease and
soothes and comforts the spirit.
Many scientific studies have found that through the
action of powerful natural antioxidants, tea truly
does have the ability to protect the body from ail-
ments. Both green teas and black teas have similar
benefits, although if you are drinking a cup before

bedtime, you might prefer a decaffeinated variety.

It is hard for most of us, so blessed with a bath-room of our own, to believe that our parents or grandparents grew up without such a room at all. My mother once told me that my grandfather did not think it proper to have the "outhouse" *in* the house! Grandmother, with her flair for Victorian dec-orating, finally persuaded him to build one on the inside. Back then, people thought it nice to have a room dedicated to the bath, but to put a toilet in the house was quite another thing. My grandmother decorated her bath with beribboned wallpaper and cabbage rose linoleum rugs. Displayed in my bath today are her blue and white bowl and water pitcher, gentle reminders of days gone by.

The bath has evolved from just an ordinary room to a kind of private sanctuary, where we can take refuge from the stresses and strains of the modern world.

Walk into any mall or even a large city airport, and you will find store after store dedicated to the art of pampering—The Body Shop®, Body Works®, Victoria's Secret®, and Bath and Body®, just to name a few. Each one sells tempting bottles of lotions, gels, creams, and oils that add comfort to our time in the bath. As a business traveler, I like to spend a little extra time in my hotel room pampering myself. Here I am physically removed

A Place for Indulgence

Whenever you need a refreshing pick-me-up, you can pretend that your home is a luxurious hotel or spa and treat yourself to an evening of pampering. Select some lotions, creams, perfumes, bath oils, soaps, dusting powders, bath salts, or sachets in your favorite fragrances. Set out extra large fluffy white towels, which feel velvety to the touch, in the bathroom. Scent your sheets and pillows with linen spray. Float rose petals in the bath water or add a few drops of essential oil. Sip flavored sparkling water in a stemmed glass and indulge in a few decadent chocolates. Enjoy a taste of the sublime as you listen to the quiet.

from the responsibilities of day-to-day life at home. Some hotels offer professional day spa services, but a fluffy terrycloth robe stretched out on the foot of my bed and a fragrant bath running work just fine for me. Wrapping the robe around my shoulders, I

For the winter is past, the rain is over and gone. The flowers are springing up and the time of the singing of birds has come.

SONG OF SOLOMON
2:11-12

step away from the day's work and into a world of serenity and gentility.

I have even started traveling with my own bottle of linen spray that I use to scent the pillows and sheets when I turn back the covers of the bed. Linen spray is also a thoughtful touch at home for you or for overnight guests. Its clean, fresh fragrance makes it seem as though the sheets have been hanging in the outside air and are fresh off the line. Time away from home always leaves me longing for a familiar, personal touch. Because smell is the strongest of our senses, spraying my pillow with a comforting scent leaves me with dreams of home. Add a few drops of perfume to a lamp on the dresser and it too will fill the room with fragrance.

Take in the scents of beauty and indulge yourself in calmness as you treat yourself to a time of pampering.

At-Home Spa Treatments

Morning Facial Treat

- 🌸 1 white washcloth
- 🌸 fresh herbal sprigs

Wet your washcloth with hot water. Place a sprig of rosemary, chamomile, or lavender in the center. Fold over the washcloth and wring out any excess water to release the herbal fragrance into the steam of the washcloth. Lay the washcloth over your face and breathe in deeply. Enjoy until the cloth cools. As a summer treat, I keep a mini bouquet of rosemary in a crystal bud vase by my bathroom sink so it is handy every morning.

The Touch of a Sponge

For a spot of luxury in the bath, fill a wicker basket with assorted sponges. Sea sponges and their velvety texture are great for absorbing water. Loofa sponges are wonderful to use for exfoliating with bath salts. Let sponges dry thoroughly between use to prevent mold and mildew. You can clean them by soaking in the sink with a tablespoon of bleach.

Relaxing Spa Bath Salts

Give yourself permission to disappear from the world while using my favorite bath salt recipe. Find a pretty seashell or a demitasse cup to use as a scoop.

- 2 cups Epsom salts
- 1 teaspoon almond oil
- lavender essential oil
- sprigs of dried lavender

Combine all ingredients in a large mixing bowl until well blended. Store in an airtight container. When ready to use, pour some salts into the middle of a wet washcloth and sit on the side of the tub, massaging your feet with the mixture. Then pour two heaping scoops under running water and slip all the way into the tub to enjoy. The lavender fragrance is so wonderful!

Pretty jars found at tag sales make perfect containers for bath salts. If the jars do not have lids, you can use a piece of cork instead. If giving pretty bath salts as a gift, dip a piece of cork in colored melted wax (color with crayons) on the bottle and use it to seal your gift.

Luxury Milk Bath

- 🌹 1 cup cornstarch
- 🌹 2 cups dry milk powder
- 🌹 1/4 teaspoon almond fragrance oil

Combine dry ingredients in food processor or blender until mixed well. Add almond oil and mix again. Upon bathing, add one half cup to hot running water for a luxurious and fragrant bath treat.

Delicious Vanilla

Vanilla seems to be the number-one choice of the fragrance world. Its calming fragrance is soothing to our souls, whether in a scrumptious ice cream cone or in a luxurious bath. You can easily make your own vanilla shower gel. Add 2 teaspoons vanilla perfume oil and 1 3/4 teaspoon apricot perfume oil to 1 cup of unscented shower gel. Stir together until blended well.

Spa Facial Steam

Create a facial steam tent by draping a bath-size towel over your head and placing a bowl of steaming herbs below. A handful of fresh mint steeped in hot water is energizing while lavender and chamomile help you to relax. If fresh herbs are unavailable, use drops of essential oil in the steaming water. Have a glass of ice water with sliced lemon nearby to sip when you are finished with your facial.

Secret Fizzing Bath Formula

- 1 cup baking soda
- 1/2 cup citric acid
- 1/2 cup cornstarch
- 30 drops essential oil (rosemary, lavender, or citrus)
- 3 drops yellow food coloring
- 3 drops blue food coloring

Combine dry ingredients in a mixing bowl. Pour into a food processor, adding the food coloring as desired. You may have to experiment and adjust your drops according to the type of food coloring used, but try to attain an azure blue-green color. Pour back into the mixing bowl and add the essential oil. Stir well. Run tap water until hot and sprinkle two scoops of salts into the water. Ease into the tub and relax.

Rosemary and Oatmeal Body Scrub

Oatmeal is wonderful to smooth, soften, and exfoliate sensitive skin.

- 1 cup uncooked oatmeal (not instant)
- 1 cup dried rose petals
- 1/2 cup blanched almonds
- 1/2 cup dried lemon peels

Mix all ingredients in food processor or blender until texture is fine. Pour into a pretty crystal jar with a lid, and leave by the side of the tub with a coffee scoop. When in the tub and ready to use it, pour a full scoop into the center of a wet washcloth and rub in a circular motion on wet skin to smooth and exfoliate.

Listen to Your Surroundings

Joys come from simple and natural things:
Mists over meadows, sunlight on leaves,
the path of the moon over the water.

SIGURD F. OLSON

e can enrich our lives by listening to our surroundings. My family and I have chosen to live in the country because it is where we are the happiest. I am most at peace when I am close to nature and it is close to me. The summer sounds of the whippoorwill, the autumn wind rustling through the branches of our red oak trees, and little boys' laughter as they roll down a hill of spring grass are some of my favorite sounds.

I love the simple happenings of the country. Last night we welcomed a newcomer to our neighborhood. Across the highway from where we live, a baby colt was born. My husband and I walked across the road and stood, one foot propped on the lower rail of the crossbuck fence, resting our chins on folded arms. We

Even the tiniest of kitchen windows can be brightened with a feeder that attracts birds of the area. Keep your feeders full of sunflower seeds and thistle mix to attract a flurry of activity. Place a cozy chair by the window and drape it with a luxurious lap throw, and bring out the binoculars and a field guide for bird identification. You can also plant a variety of shrubs and bushes to attract specific visitors to your window. Azaleas, lupines, and pansies are some of my favorites. Study gardening catalogs to find out which plants are best for your area. Add a birdbath to watch the playfulness of robins splashing. From woodpeckers to bluebirds, a gray rainy day can be brightened considerably by a visit from feathered friends.

gazed intently at filly and three-day-old foal standing side by side, one of life's incredible miracles. All of the neighbors watching took note of this special moment as the new mother gently licked and nuzzled her baby. The evening shadows had grown long when the owner came out to turn on the barn light and invite us into the stall. Amid the fresh hay lay mother and foal, close enough for us to touch. The softness of the foal's velvety new fur, the flick of her short little tail, and the licking of her tongue on my hand melted my heart. My husband had to gently pull me away to leave, for I think I could have stood there all night, watching mother and child. This was such a beautiful moment spent listening to the quiet, outdoors with God's magnificent creation.

For most of us, solitude in our surroundings is not easy to find. However, we can create a place of relaxation just beyond our bedroom door. As we learn to momentarily step back from the tension of our day-to-day schedules, we can delight in our own oasis of quiet. We can be alone with God as we

The beautiful is as useful as the useful. Perhaps more so.

VICTOR HUGO

Outdoor Lemonade Sipper

- 🌹 1 12-ounce can ginger ale
- 🌹 1 cup sugar
- 🌹 5 cups cold water
- 🌹 8 lemons, juiced

Combine all ingredients in a large pitcher and chill. Serve in a stemmed glass garnished with a strawberry on the rim. For a quicker version, you can substitute a can of frozen lemonade concentrate made according to directions. Just add the ginger ale.

rekindle our glow from within and replenish our well that has become depleted.

One way to replenish our well is to surround our senses with beauty. Fragrance makes such a personal statement in our homes and surroundings, and it is just as important as color, for we can close our eyes and not see color, but we cannot staying at home for real comfort," says the author Jane Austen. As a special treat on weekends, I love to plump up the pillows and turn back the bed covers as an invitation to retire at my leisure. Even if I am unable to take a nap that day, I enjoy seeing that the bed is ready for me when evening falls.

I recently helped a friend shop for a painting to hang in her bedroom. It would be the first thing she saw in the morning, as her window had no view. Most people hang a print over the head of their bed, but the only time they see it is when they are elsewhere in the room. A favorite painting is more soothing when you place it where you can see it as you drift off to

How the oriole's nest is hung,
Where the whitest lilies blow,
Where the freshest berries grow,
Where the ground-nut
trails its vine,
Where the wood-grape
clusters shine.

JOHN
GREENLEAF
WHITTIER
THE BAREFOOT BOY

sleep at night or open your eyes in the morning. My friend chose a print of a luscious basket of cascading roses. She is a gardener at heart, and the roses brought to her bedroom a sense of comfort and security, transforming it into an inner sanctuary furnished with the qualities that spoke to her soul.

The haven of escape that nurtures solitude may come in many forms—a gym, a theater, a kitchen. A favorite sport or activity can leave our minds as well as our bodies invigorated. For those who love to cook, time spent trying new recipes and puttering around the kitchen serves as a simple escape. Using a new espresso machine, making crafts, or preparing homemade bread can all be rewarding pursuits that soothe the soul. If we invest in time away from the world of the ordinary and the routine, we will receive better clarity and a restored sense of balance.

Whether you live in the city or the country, the skies everywhere are filled with the beauty of God's delightful creatures. My dainty little mother-in-law doesn't get out of her house very much, as a broken hip has made walking difficult, but she delights in the activities of her visiting hummingbirds. From her window, she watches as they arrive in the spring, enjoy an offering of nectar from the feeders in the summer, and then depart come fall. Some days she tallies their attendance and delights in sharing this news. Whether from a condominium window or a country kitchen view, observing God's creation is soothing to the soul as you listen to your surroundings. Drink in the beauty and be renewed.

Listen to Something New

*Open thou mine eyes, that I
may behold wondrous things...*

PSALM 119:18

Experiencing something new can expand
our horizons and give us a renewed
excitement for life. Visiting new places, trying new
restaurants, reading new books, and meeting new
people all allow fresh perspectives to be born.
Learning to do something you've always been
interested in doing opens up new possibilities.
A change of pace from the daily routine can be as
simple as having a spontaneous picnic beside a
stream or driving home a different way from work.
Whatever you choose to do, you'll make new
discoveries in how to live and how to see the world.

In trying something new, we can renew ourselves. For twenty-six years my husband and I have
lived in the same house. It has taken years of hard
work to restore this turn-of-the-century home to its
former glory. The initial restoration took detective
work on our part to discover the home's original
details and color scheme. We tried valiantly to keep
everything the same as it had originally been,

Something to Look Forward To

Just as the finest of hotels spoil guests with chocolate on their pillows, you can introduce this luxury at home. Purchase an outrageously decadent piece of chocolate and save it for your special quiet time of the day, perhaps after everyone else is asleep in the closing moments of your evening.

including refusing to move a pitiful-looking rose bush that struggled to put forth blooms under an oak tree. We knew that the rose bush was quite old because its canes were so large, but it rarely put out roses. Still, it was original to the home, so we felt obligated to keep it.

I didn't want to move the rose bush because under the oak tree was where it was originally planted. However, one day while workers were installing a new sprinkler system, necessity forced me to move it. One of the fellows digging observed that when the bush had first been planted there, it enjoyed full sun. The oak tree was just a sapling back then, but now it shaded the entire south side of the house with its huge out-stretched limbs.

We moved the rose bush in front of the old carriage house to a spot in the sun and this allowed the bush to thrive. That was two years ago. Its canes now reach to the

carriage house roof and bloom with the most generous profusion of roses I could ever imagine.

Once more on my adventure brave and new.

ROBERT BROWNING

Allowing for a change gave the rose bush a new lease on life. Sometimes we need to be like the rose bush. Often we merely need to get away for a change, to step out of our daily routine, to become revitalized. Our scheduled tasks can be performed with newfound enthusiasm when we take a moment to step out of our cycle and become rested and renewed by something different.

Sometimes the something new can be the simplest of activities. One of my favorite childhood memories is eating a peanut butter sandwich picnic lunch on our back door steps. Mother told me early in the morning that we would have a picnic and eat our lunch outside that day. I looked forward to lunchtime with great anticipation! Our picnic happened just on the doorstep, mere feet away from the chrome and Formica kitchen table we normally ate at. Yet doing an ordinary activity in a different place made it an event.

A few years ago I was in New York City alone on a business trip. I was so unhappy because my meeting that day had not turned out the way I hoped it would. However, business was finished for the day and my hotel was right in the middle of the acclaimed theater district, so I decided to pick up my spirits by seeing if I could get a last-minute ticket to a Broadway play. Sometimes spontaneous decisions are the best ones of all, and my spontaneous decision to go to the theater turned the not-so-successful trip into a favorite memory.

Variety's the source of joy below, From whence still fresh revolving pleasures flow. In books and love, the mind one end pursues, And only change th'expiring flame renews.

JOHN GAY

One of the shows playing on Broadway was *The Secret Garden.* Tickets were sold out, but as luck would have it several people had not picked up their tickets and I became the proud new occupant of a third-row seat. Seating herself ten minutes before curtain time, the well-dressed lady next to me was also by herself and had had the same good fortune in securing her last-minute ticket. We exchanged business cards and photos of our children, and then *The Secret Garden* began with an orchestral burst of kettledrums. Mesmerized by story and song, I let the music and acting sweep me away to another time and place. I don't recall the name of the important person I'd had the important meeting with earlier that day. But I do remember I left the theater that

Water Therapy

Water has always been restorative to the soul, whether we bathe in it or simply enjoy the sensation of it. Here are some favorite ideas for letting water nurture you.

- *Take a walk in the rain.*
- *Walk barefoot on the beach and let the waves caress your toes.*
- *Take off your shoes and socks and dip your feet in the cold water of a rushing stream.*
- *Swim at night. Moonlight on the shimmering water is so peaceful.*
- *Stroll around a lake.*
- *At a party, slip off your shoes and put your feet in the pool.*
- *Sip ice water with lots of lemon in a stemmed goblet.*
- *Fill your bathtub with water and float candles in it.*
- *Freeze a (plastic) bottle of water and carry it with you on hot summer days.*
- *Learn to skip a rock on a pond.*
- *Use rainwater as a final rinse on your hair.*

Quiet Tips

🌹 Sugar shakers make pretty holders for dusting powder.

🌹 Miniature roses are charming in old, chipped teacups.

🌹 Keep your favorite body spritzer in the refrigerator for a cool and refreshing splash of fragrance.

🌹 Tuck a small sachet under your pillow for sweet dreams.

Simple but True

Baking soda and salt make the best toothpaste ever!

🌹 1 teaspoon baking soda

🌹 1 teaspoon salt

Mix soda and salt in the palm of your hand. As a former dental hygienist, I can assure you that using this recipe will result in healthy teeth and gums.

night humming, refreshed and enriched by the evening's performance.

When you become interested in something, your life takes on a rosier glow. I get so frustrated when my sons complain, "I'm bored. I don't have anything to do." Yet even we adults can get into a rut that creates boredom and self-centeredness. To escape from it, we must care about and show concern for others and do something new. Our reward will come back to us as soothing contentment.

A lady at my church, who must now be in her seventies, is one of the most youthful people I know. Mrs. Shiras is constantly volunteering at the local homeless shelter, sorting canned goods at the food bank, delivering meals to shut-ins, and even playing the piano early on Sunday mornings at the Salvation Army. She has traveled to the Holy Land many times and enthusiastically shares her experiences when asked to speak. Her busy schedule demands that she make the most of her time, and last week she even asked me for my e-mail address! I find myself looking forward to chatting with her, as she is so interesting. In fact, the lessons I learn at church are not just from the sermons. They are often from Mrs. Shiras and her contagious enthusiasm for life.

O sing unto the Lord a new song; for he hath done marvellous things.

PSALM 98:1

When we get interested in other people, places, and things, we become more interesting. When we engage in something new, our whole world blossoms.

Renaissance

A thing of beauty is a joy for ever:
Its loveliness increases; it will never
Pass into nothingness; but still will keep
A bower quiet for us, and a sleep
Full of sweet dreams, and health, and quiet breathing.

JOHN KEATS

The French gave us the word "renaissance," which means a renewal and rebirth of the old. Now more than ever, we are in need of a renaissance. The roads we travel in our lifetime make us who we are, and at times we need to look back and reflect on where we've come from. It is so easy to get caught up in the day-to-day busy work of today and tomorrow. Yet it is ever so important that we stop and listen to the quiet.

We are all blessed with the ability to open new doors and discover old ones. As I have traveled along, I have discovered that there is truth in the saying, "Joy is not just a destination, but it is the journey along the way." This saying reminds me of a very special couple I met on my summer vacation several years ago.

Stationed along the interstate every so many miles is a rest stop for weary travelers. Those of us on long trips truly appreciate these stops, as they allow us to take a break from the mesmerizing hum and cramped confines of the car. In some areas of the country, volunteers offer free coffee at roadsides along the way. I have fond memories of one such couple—a husband and wife who shared their holidays with others. They had lost their daughter to a drunk driver, and this was their way of healing the hurt. They offered warm coffee and smiles that ministered to those in need and a safe rest to those who were simply weary. I was so impressed by their response to tragedy. I know that their sweet spirit will remain with me forever.

Within the realm of renewal and renaissance, each of our roads has many twists and turns. No matter who we are, where we live, or what we do, we all have a need to be still and listen to the quiet as we journey on our way. With the gentle art of nourishing our souls, listening to the quiet helps us to be better mothers, better daughters, better friends, better sisters, and better wives tomorrow than we are today.